3-8-04

X

Hampshire County
Public Library

D1212891

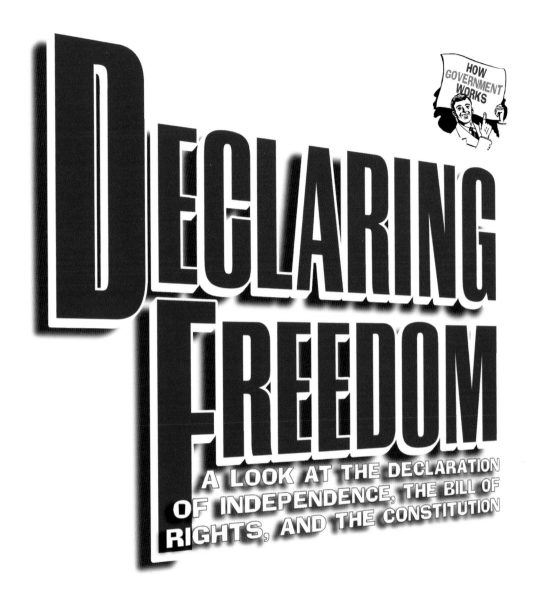

DECLARING FREEDOM

A LOOK AT THE DECLARATION OF INDEPENDENCE, THE BILL OF RIGHTS, AND THE CONSTITUTION

By Gwenyth Swain

LERNER PUBLICATIONS COMPANY • MINNEAPOLIS

Copyright © 2004 by Gwenyth Swain

All rights reserved. International copyright secured. No part of this book may be reproduced, stored in a retrieval system, or transmitted in any form or by any means—electronic, mechanical, photocopying, recording, or otherwise—without the prior written permission of Lerner Publications Company, except for the inclusion of brief quotations in an acknowledged review.

Lerner Publications Company
A division of Lerner Publishing Group
241 First Avenue North
Minneapolis, MN 55401 U.S.A.

Website address: www.lernerbooks.com

Library of Congress Cataloging-in-Publication Data

Swain, Gwenyth, 1961–
    Declaring freedom : a look at the Declaration of Independence, the Bill of
Rights, and the Constitution / by Gwenyth Swain.
       p.   cm. — (How government works)
    Includes bibliographical references and index.
    Summary: Explores the origin, meaning, and importance of the Declaration
of Independence, the Constitution, and the Bill of Rights.
    ISBN: 0–8225–1348–X (lib. bdg. : alk. paper)
    1. United States. Declaration of Independence—Juvenile literature.
2. United States. Constitution—Juvenile literature. 3. United States.
Constitution. 1st–10th Amendments—Juvenile literature. 4. United States—
Politics and government—1775–1783—Juvenile literature. 5. United States—
Politics and government—1783–1789—Juvenile literature. [1. United States.
Declaration of Independence. 2. United States. Constitution. 3. United
States. Constitution. 1st–10th Amendments. 4. United States—Politics
and government—1775–1783. 5. United States—Politics and government—
1783–1789.] I. Title. II. Series.
E221.S94 2004
973.3'1—dc21   2003005609

Manufactured in the United States of America
1 2 3 4 5 6 – DP – 09 08 07 06 05 04

TABLE OF CONTENTS

INTRODUCTION: THE CHARTERS OF FREEDOM

QUICK QUESTION: What do the Declaration of Independence, the U.S. Constitution, and the Bill of Rights have in common? They share one name: the Charters of Freedom. They are also on display in the National Archives building in Washington, D.C. More than one million people visit the Charters of Freedom every year.

Why make such a fuss over pieces of paper and parchment, covered with

The Charters of Freedom, at more than two hundred years old, have been carefully preserved for viewing.

faded brown ink? The answer lies in their name: the Charters of Freedom. A charter is a document on paper, papyrus, or parchment. But *charter* comes from the Latin word *charta*, which means "map." Think of these three documents as road maps to our freedom. Without them, American democracy wouldn't exist.

This is the story of how we got these three road maps to freedom. It's a story about a frustrated group of thirteen colonies, a stubborn king, and a long, hard war. And finally, it's a story about the desire for freedom and liberty. That desire was made stronger by all the challenges it met.

When does the story begin? It's hard to say exactly. But if you look back to America in the 1760s, you won't be far off.

COLONIAL ROLL CALL

Just what were the thirteen original American Colonies? New Hampshire, Massachusetts, Connecticut, and Rhode Island were the New England Colonies. The Middle Colonies were New York, New Jersey, Pennsylvania, and Delaware. Virginia and Maryland were colonies in the Chesapeake Bay area. Farther south were North Carolina, South Carolina, and Georgia. Many of these colonies had been set up in part to allow people living in them to practice whatever religion they pleased.

CHAPTER 1
WHY BE INDEPENDENT?

TRUE OR FALSE? American colonists loved King George III of Great Britain. The answer is False.

If you were an American colonist in the late 1700s, you were probably tired and angry and frustrated, or fed up. Many colonists were tired of being bullied by their king, George III. Just like people living in Britain, the colonists had to put up with King George's orders and decrees, even if they were unfair.

Many colonists were angry that Great Britain's Parliament (lawmak-

> American colonists met to discuss their dissatisfaction with British rule.

ing and taxing body) passed laws that the colonists had no say in. Unlike people living in Britain, people living in the colonies weren't allowed to elect members of Britain's Parliament. They simply had to put up with whatever taxes and laws Parliament passed. At least the colonists had always done so before.

In March 1765, Parliament passed the Stamp Act, a tax on paper goods. That's when some people in America's thirteen colonies became so frustrated with Parliament and the king that they decided not to put up with things as usual anymore.

Stamps *(top right)* showed that the tax on paper goods had been paid. Some colonists were so mad about the tax that they protested in the streets *(above)*.

NO TAXATION WITHOUT REPRESENTATION!

Americans in the 1700s complained loudly when Britain taxed them. American colonists couldn't elect members of Parliament, where taxes such as the Stamp Act of 1765 were decided. Colonists called this taxation without representation.

Britain needed to pay for fighting a recent war with France in North America. Shouldn't American colonists help repay the war debt, Parliament asked? Couldn't colonists pay more for paper goods?

To Americans, the Stamp Act was outrageous. They protested. They signed petitions, or written requests demanding changes. They complained so long and loud that in February 1766, the Stamp Act was repealed, and the tax was ended.

In this early 1770s drawing, the citizens of Boston, Massachusetts, torment a British tax collector by covering him with tar and feathers and by forcing him to drink British tea.

IT'S INTOLERABLE!

Americans rejoiced, but not for long. Other taxes followed. One was on tea. You may think tea is bitter and nasty, but colonists loved it. Once Britain started taxing tea, however, many Americans stopped drinking it.

Colonial women spun their own thread for homespun cloth after Britain began taxing linen and silk cloth.

HOMESPUN HEROINES

When Britain started taxing colonists, girls and women formed groups called Daughters of Liberty. In Edenton, North Carolina, more than fifty Daughters declared that they would no longer use British tea or cloth. Sassafras roots and chamomile made fine "liberty tea." They and their families would wear clothes made of homespun cloth woven on their very own looms at home. Other Daughters of Liberty throughout the colonies did the same. They even held spinning bees, where they spun thread for weaving into cloth.

They boiled roots and herbs for tea instead.

Then, one night in 1773, a group of colonists crept onto a ship in Boston Harbor. They threw tons of tea into the harbor to show how fed up they were. Had Americans gone too far? Britain thought so. British officials turned homes upside down because they suspected colonists of smuggling tea— and avoiding taxes. British soldiers smashed or shut down American printing presses that criticized the king.

In 1774 Parliament passed laws to punish Americans.

Colonists dumped tea into Boston Harbor. This was called the Boston Tea Party.

LEARN THE LINGO

Intolerable is a great word to use when describing things you don't like. It means "unbearable." Try using it on your little brother or big sister when he or she is being a pest. You'll know just how the colonists felt after Parliament passed the Intolerable Acts in 1774.

Boston Harbor was shut down until Bostonians paid for the tea they'd pitched into the water. Parliament reorganized the Massachusetts colony's government so the people had less power. Parliament also said that the colony's governor could place British troops in homes and other private buildings. Colonists hated these laws, but they couldn't do a thing about them.

These laws were called the Coercive Acts, but Americans called them "intolerable." The Intolerable Acts made Americans even angrier than the Stamp Act had. The Stamp Act had been just a tax. This time Parliament was trying to pass laws for the colonies, laws in which the colonists had no voice.

TIME FOR CHANGE

Americans grew so angry they chose a few people from each of the thirteen different colonies to go to a meeting, called the Continental Congress. When they met in Philadelphia, Pennsylvania, in September 1774, most still hoped that things could be put right with Britain. But in April 1775, British troops went looking for muskets and gunpowder. Massachusetts colonists in the militia (troops first organized to fight Great Britain's war against France) had stored the ammunition. Some militia members were so angry they were ready to use it to fight against Britain. No one knows who fired the first shots in Lexington and Concord. But in those Massachusetts towns and on the

Massachusetts militia members exchanged fire with British troops in Lexington, Massachusetts, in April 1775.

Britain's King George III was a stubborn ruler who did not easily give in to the demands of his subjects.

road to Boston as the British retreated, both colonists and redcoats died. (British soldiers were known as redcoats because they wore red uniforms.)

That August, George III said what many colonists already knew. The Americans were in rebellion against their king.

Still, most colonists didn't want to be independent. They wanted things to be the way they used to be— back when the king and Parliament weren't always taxing the colonists. Back when colonists enjoyed more freedom.

It took a writer and former corset maker to change American views on independence. His name was Thomas Paine. Paine didn't go in for long, fancy words or Latin quotations. King George III was, in his words, "the Royal Brute of Britain." In 1776 Paine's pamphlet *Common Sense* became an instant best-seller. It called for complete

"SOUND BYTE" "For God's sake, let us come to a final separation. . . . The birthday of a new world is at hand."
—Thomas Paine, 1776

independence from Great Britain. Someone came up with a snappy slogan, and posters up and down the colonies promised "Common Sense for eighteen pence!"

Eighteen pence was cheap. If only Americans could gain their freedom at such a bargain price. But the struggle for liberty would cost much more.

In *Common Sense,* Thomas Paine made important arguments for American independence from Britain.

COMMON SENSE;

ADDRESSED TO THE

INHABITANTS

OF

AMERICA,

On the following interesting

SUBJECTS.

I. Of the Origin and Design of Government in general, with concise Remarks on the English Constitution.

II. Of Monarchy and Hereditary Succession.

IIh Thoughts on the present State of American Affairs.

IV. Of the present Ability of America, with some miscellaneous Reflections.

A NEW EDITION, with several Additions in the Body of the Work. To which is added an APPENDIX; together with an Address to the People called QUAKERS.

N P. The New Addition here given increases the Work upward of one Third.

Man knows no Master save creating HEAVEN,
Or those whom Choice and common Good ordain.
THOMSON.

PHILADELPHIA PRINTED.
And SOLD by W and T BRADFORD

The Second Continental Congress met in Philadelphia, in Pennsylvania's statehouse. The building later became known as Independence Hall.

The first big step in that struggle was to make it clear that colonists were no longer going to put up with things as usual. More and more of them wanted independence.

Men from all over the colonies had gathered in Philadelphia for the Second Continental Congress. They had come together to govern the colonies in the struggle with Britain. And in the summer of 1776, they made a declaration about independence. In the process, they made history too.

CHAPTER 2
THE DECLARATION OF INDEPENDENCE

TRUE OR FALSE? Freedom is easy. False! It's hard work! Sometimes it's smelly and sweaty too.

Thomas Jefferson didn't want to be in Philadelphia in the summer of 1776. The weather was hot. Clouds of flies hung over the smelly streets. But the Second Continental Congress was meeting there, and Jefferson was a

America's founders signed the Declaration of Independence in 1776.

"**SOUND** "These are the
    BYTE" times that try
men's souls."
—Thomas Paine,
    1776

delegate, one of the people speaking for the colony of Virginia.

On June 7, 1776, Richard Henry Lee, another Virginia delegate, made a motion, or a formal statement. He resolved "That these United Colonies are . . . free and independent States. . . . " Jefferson and other congressmen debated Lee's motion. Should they support it? Should they reconcile with Britain or declare independence?

Congress could not make up its mind. Finally, it did what it still does when its members can't agree. It set up a committee.

Thomas Jefferson was on the committee. He joined old Benjamin Franklin of Pennsylvania, Roger Sherman of Connecticut, New Yorker Robert R. Livingston, and short, stout John Adams of Massachusetts. Together, the men were called the Committee of Five.

By the middle of 1776, many colonists were ready to declare themselves independent from

The Committee of Five put their heads together to declare American independence.

In June 1776, Thomas Jefferson worked hard to draft the Declaration of Independence.

Britain. The committee asked Jefferson to write a draft declaration about American independence. A draft is an early version of a text—one that's meant to be reworked before it's made public.

Jefferson worked fast. On June 28, Jefferson brought a draft before the Congress. Congress was busy. The Continental Army under General George Washington was preparing for bigger battles in the Revolutionary War. Any reading and tinkering with Jefferson's declaration had to be done after the business of war was taken care of. Still, the Congress took its job seriously. Members worked over Jefferson's draft until it was a polished Declaration of Independence—the one we still celebrate.

What does it say? In a nutshell, the Declaration announces the Continental Congress's decision to become independent from Britain and form a new nation. It lists the

PEOPLE FILE When Thomas Jefferson decided what would go on his tombstone, he didn't mention being our third president. Instead, the first thing he wanted written in stone was "Author of the Declaration of American Independence."

The Declaration of Independence, signed by fifty-six delegates to the Continental Congress, led to historic change.

reasons why independence is necessary. The former colonists—later to be called Americans—"declare the causes which impel [force] them to the Separation." (*Separation* is another word for independence.)

Before listing the reasons for separation, the Declaration of Independence has a paragraph full of great ideas. One of those ideas is that good government gets its power from the people, or "from the Consent of the Governed." In other words, a good government listens to its citizens.

WHO'S CREATED EQUAL?

The Declaration of Independence says, "We hold these Truths to be self-evident, that all Men are created equal. . . . " What do these thirteen words mean? Jefferson probably meant that no one person is better than another. You might be born a king, for example, but that doesn't make you better than a corset maker.

The words *seem* to promise equal rights to all Americans. That's how many people understand the words. But in 1776, most blacks in America were slaves. The rights of Indians to live on their lands were not respected. American women couldn't vote, and most couldn't own property.

Since 1776 many groups have worked to make real the equality promised in those thirteen words. In 1848, when Elizabeth Cady Stanton started fighting for women's rights, she copied the Declaration. But she added a twist, writing "We hold these truths to be self-evident: that all men *and women* are created equal."

Even though the Declaration of Independence said all men were created equal, black slaves did not have the same rights as white men.

It gives them a voice in making laws. When Britain passed the Intolerable Acts, it didn't ask for the colonists' consent. When colonists complained, King George III didn't listen to them. That kind of government—one that doesn't ask your consent or listen when you complain—is bad government. The Declaration of Independence says Americans have the right to get rid of a bad government and create a new one.

The Declaration also lists things the king did to Americans, all of which make it "their Duty, to throw off such a Government." Most troubling was this charge against the king: "He is, at this Time, transporting large Armies of his foreign Mercenaries to compleat [complete] works of Death, Desolation, and Tyranny. . . ." *The British were coming!* An army of professional, paid soldiers

British troops arrived in New York City in the summer of 1776.

In some areas where most people favored independence from Britain, Americans loyal to the British were run out of town.

WHERE DO YOUR LOYALTIES LIE?

Not all colonists supported the war. Some felt stronger ties to Britain, the mother country, than they did to the colony where they lived. Quite a few thought of themselves as British first, Pennsylvanian or Virginian second. Even more colonists were loyal to both sides. When troops of the Continental Army were in town, these colonists were patriots. When British redcoats came, these colonists dusted off their portraits of King George III. Some called them "sunshine patriots." General George Washington called them "abominable pests." But their willingness to change sides reflected the divided loyalties of many colonists. They loved their mother country. But most loved liberty even more.

(mercenaries) was already on its way to American shores.

All this was happening after Americans had tried to get the British government to hear their complaints. Many colonists were from Britain. Most considered themselves to be British. But the British hadn't listened to the colonists' complaints. (As the Declaration puts it, they'd been "deaf to the Voice of Justice.") So Americans would have to consider the British their enemies. At least for now. "We must . . . ," the Declaration states, "hold them, as we hold the rest of Mankind, Enemies in War, in Peace, Friends."

It took Congress many paragraphs to give all its reasons for seeking independence. Then, in one last paragraph, the authors pulled out the stops. Here, Americans make that final declaration: "We . . . solemnly Publish and Declare, That these United Colonies are, and by Right ought to be, FREE AND INDEPENDENT STATES. . . ."

"PUT YOUR JOHN HANCOCK HERE!"

Ever heard this expression? It goes back to the Second Continental Congress. John Hancock was the president of the Congress. When the Declaration of Independence was approved on July 4, 1776, Hancock signed it as Congress's president. Other congressmen did not start signing the Declaration until it had been copied onto parchment in August. Again, John Hancock signed first. As you can see, he had a pretty impressive signature.

John Hancock put the original "John Hancock" (a large signature) on the Declaration of Independence in 1776.

Braving snow and ice, Washington and his troops crossed the Delaware River to attack British forces at Trenton, New Jersey, in December 1776.

Congress took just three days to discuss the Declaration before approving it on July 4, 1776. What followed were seven long years of war.

GOING TO WAR

At first, General George Washington and the Continental Army met with defeat after defeat. The army's first major victory was a surprise attack on Christmas night. Washington ordered his men to cross the freezing Delaware River. As dawn broke, Continental forces surrounded sleepy soldiers fighting for Britain.

SNOWSHOES AT VALLEY FORGE

Few Native Americans sided with the colonists in their war with Britain. Most believed the British would better protect native lands. Still, some Indians did support the Americans. During the long, snowy winter of 1777 to 1778, the Oneida of New York sent two hundred pairs of much-needed snowshoes to Continental forces at Valley Forge in Pennsylvania.

Some months later, America lost its most important city, Philadelphia, to the British. The Revolutionary War was like that: a small victory here, a big loss there. Winters were spent trying not to freeze and starve. Summers were spent trying not to die from spoiled food or from a musket shot.

The war dragged on. In the end, both sides tired of fighting, but Britain was more tired. In 1783 the Americans and the British signed a treaty. That treaty did two important things. It ended a long, hard war. It also confirmed what Americans had said in the Declaration of Independence seven years before: We are no longer colonies of Britain. We are a group of independent states.

Maybe a little too independent. Some Americans worried that war wasn't their biggest problem. Would staying together in peacetime be an even bigger struggle?

We the People of the United States, in order to form a more perfect Union, establish Justice, insure domestic Tranquility, provide for the common defence, promote the general Welfare, and secure the Blessings of Liberty to ourselves and our Posterity, do ordain and establish this Constitution for the United States of America.

Article I.

Section. 1. All legislative Powers herein granted shall be vested in a Congress of the United States, which shall consist of a Senate and House of Representatives.

Section. 2. The House of Representatives shall be composed of Members chosen every second Year by the People of the several States, and the Electors in each State shall have the Qualifications requisite for Electors of the most numerous Branch of the State Legislature.

CHAPTER 3
AN AMERICAN CONSTITUTION

QUICK QUESTION: What was America's first government like? It was a mess—a big mess.

Its powers were spelled out in the Articles of Confederation, written in 1777 and approved in 1781. Under the Articles, the thirteen states didn't act much like the United States of America. They acted independently, like little countries. States passed laws. The Confederation congress couldn't. States could ask citizens to pay taxes. Congress could only make suggestions and requests. Most states printed their own paper money, and each kind was different.

> The U.S. Constitution strengthened the bonds among the thirteen states.

Daniel Shays and His Rebellion

Many Americans suffered in the economic crisis under America's first government. Farmers, in particular, were paid such low prices for their crops that they could barely make a living. Daniel Shays, a captain in the Revolutionary War, grew angry when his fellow farmers began losing their land. In 1786 Shays led two thousand farmers in Massachusetts in a rebellion. Shays's rebels closed down courthouses and nearly captured a storehouse for guns and ammunition. Shays's Rebellion ended in defeat in 1787, but it got people's attention. Many believed that America's government had to be changed. Some argued that if the central government were stronger, it would be better able to keep order. A stronger government might even be able to fix problems, such as low farm prices or worthless paper money, before they led to fighting. Everyone agreed that changes to the Articles of Confederation were needed soon—before more rebellions took place.

A mob of frustrated farmers occupies this courthouse during Shays's Rebellion.

What's more, that paper money was worth almost nothing. The thirteen states were facing an economic crisis.

"**SOUND** "We are fast
    BYTE" verging to
anarchy and confusion!"
—George Washington to
James Madison,
November 5,
1786

SOMETHING HAS TO CHANGE

In 1786 James Madison of Virginia made a suggestion. Why not send delegates to Philadelphia to revise the Articles of Confederation? George Washington would lead the convention. By winning a difficult and costly war, the general had also won the respect of the delegates. Washington, Madison believed, could bring people together to solve their problems.

Only Rhode Island chose not to participate. Rhode Islanders worried that if the Articles were changed, the central government would become too strong.

DIG DEEPER Why is James Madison called the father of the Constitution? Probably it's because of all he did to help create our Constitution. But you could also say it's because he took good notes. Every day during the Constitutional Convention, Madison wrote down what was said. The official records were destroyed. But we still have Madison's notes.

James Madison

Virginia governor Edmund Randolph

Maybe Rhode Islanders also wanted to avoid the summer heat and flies and noise of the city. Surely, many of the fifty-five men who attended the convention regretted being stuck in a stuffy room in Philadelphia. But once they sat down together, they set in motion changes that would turn thirteen independent states into a true nation.

In Philadelphia before the convention, James Madison and other Virginians wrote a plan. The Virginia Plan didn't sound revolutionary at first. Virginia governor Edmund Randolph said the plan would show how the Articles could be "corrected and enlarged." Members of the convention sat back, ready to hear what they thought would be a few changes here and there. What they heard instead was a plan for a brand-new government.

Under the Virginia Plan, there would be a president. Congress would have two parts, or houses. Federal (national) courts would rule on matters affecting all states. States would give up some of their power, and the national government would gain some power. It would be able to tax people. It would regulate business and trade. It would make foreign policy decisions, decisions about how to deal with other countries.

On the surface, what the government proposed in the Virginia Plan sounds much like our modern government. But there were quite a few wrinkles to be worked out during that long, hot summer in Philadelphia. From May to September, delegates debated and drafted the U.S. Constitution.

Delegates worried that they would never agree on anything if the public listened in. So they put guards at the doors of Pennsylvania's statehouse (later renamed Independence Hall). Even in the summer heat, they nailed the windows shut. That way no one on the street could

Bearing the heat for the sake of democracy, delegates crafted the Constitution.

THREE-FIFTHS OF A PERSON

The Constitutional Convention agreed that representation in the House of Representatives should be based on population. Members also agreed that slaves should be counted as less than a person. Three-fifths of a person, to be precise. How could members have agreed to such a terrible thing? In 1787 many white Americans thought that blacks were less than human. In 1787 delegates from thirteen states had to agree on representation, or the nation might be lost. Most slaves lived in southern states. In the northern states, there were few slaves. Southern states wanted slaves to be counted as full persons, since that would give them more representatives. Northern states worried that the south would be too powerful. They didn't want slaves counted at all. In the end, both sides compromised. But arguments over slavery didn't end. They simmered for nearly one hundred years until the Civil War broke out in 1861.

hear what was being said. Delegates promised not to talk about the constitution in their lodgings or at dinner at nearby taverns.

Those closed windows and doors didn't make it easier for delegates to agree. The convention nearly broke up over how the needs of small states would be balanced with those of large states. Should states send an equal number of representatives to Congress? Many argued it would be fairest to base the number of representatives on the number of people in each state.

States with small populations protested. They wanted to be heard in the new government. Finally, the convention compromised. In one part of Congress, the House of Representatives, representation would be based on the number of people in each state. In the other part of Congress, the Senate, each state—no matter what size—

would send two representatives, or senators.

By September the delegates were exhausted. But they had done their work. They had created an outline for governing the United States. That's what a constitution is—an outline of government. The U.S. Constitution doesn't go into much detail. That's part of the secret to its success. It's like a sturdy wooden frame. We, the people, are left to fill in the details, the full picture of government in the United States.

WHAT'S AN ARTICLE?

The Constitution, presented to the convention on September 17, 1787, is only six pages long. It contains a short preamble, or opening statement. Next are seven articles. You might think these are like articles in a newspaper, but the word *article* comes from the Latin

HOUSES IN THE TREE

Article I of the Constitution describes the legislative (lawmaking) branch of government. Perched on this branch are two houses. The first is the House of Representatives. Its members are elected by the people and serve for two years. The total number of representatives is based on the population of the United States. The other house is the Senate. At first, state governments chose members of the Senate. Later, in 1913, the Constitution was changed so people could elect senators directly. Each state sends two senators, who serve for six years, to Washington, D.C. When the Constitution was written, the House of Representatives had sixty-five members, and the Senate had twenty-six. These days, the legislative branch is groaning under the weight of more than 435 representatives and one hundred senators.

BRANCHES OF THE GOVERNMENT

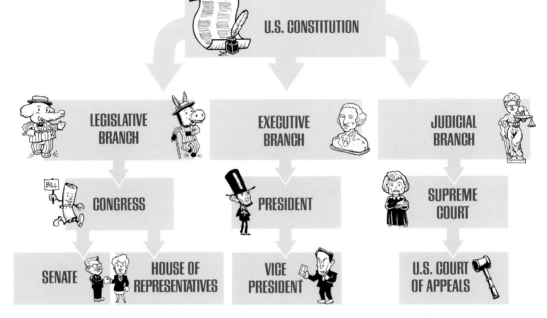

This chart shows the three branches of the U.S. government and the main parts of the branches, as described by the Constitution.

word for joint. The articles in the Constitution join the whole document together like joints connect bones in our bodies.

The first three articles show how power is divided within the government. Article I describes Congress, which is the lawmaking branch of government. Article II covers the president and vice president, who lead the executive branch. And Article III is about the federal courts and Supreme Court, which make up the judicial branch.

Nobody wanted America's president to be as strong as England's king. Nobody wanted the courts or Congress to be so powerful that they could *act* like a king. So the Constitution includes checks and balances. These are specific powers that each branch of government has over the other two. If one branch of government does something bad or illegal, another branch of government can *check*, or stop, it. No one branch is more powerful than the other. They balance each other out.

The final four articles outline the rest of our government. Article IV describes the rights and responsibilities of states. It says we can add new states and territories if we want. The Constitution looked to the future, when there might be more than thirteen states.

Article V also has the future in mind. This article allows for changes. It doesn't make changing the Constitution easy, but it does make changes possible.

Article VI is a hodgepodge. Any money owed by the United States under the Articles of Confederation, it says, is still owed by the United States under the new government. It also says that the Constitution is the "supreme Law of the Land." That's just another way of telling the states who's in charge. If the federal government passes a law that goes against a state law, the federal law prevails, or wins out. This article also says "no religious Test shall ever be required as a Qualification to any Office or public Trust under the United States." (This was not the case in Great Britain, where

"SOUND BYTE" "Like the Bible, it ought to be read again and again." —President Franklin D. Roosevelt, speaking of the Constitution in 1937

In this image, George Washington, who led the Constitutional Convention, watches as delegates sign the Constitution.

anyone who wanted to become a member of Parliament also had to be a member of the Church of England.)

The last paragraph of the Constitution, Article VII, is surprising. "The Ratification of the Conventions of nine States," it says, "shall be sufficient for the Establishment of this Constitution. . . ." In other words, only nine states had to agree to the Constitution before it went into effect. Imagine you have twelve friends over. Imagine saying that when nine of you agree to go to bed at midnight, all of you will go to bed then. You won't have to think about this for long to see that you'll get a better night's sleep if *everyone* agrees on the same bedtime. The framers of the Constitution knew this, but they realized that having nine states approve the Constitution would put pressure on all the states to fall in line.

THE FEDERALIST PAPERS

THE

FEDERALIST:

ADDRESSED TO THE

PEOPLE OF THE STATE OF NEW-YORK.

NUMBER I.

Introduction.

AFTER an unequivocal experience of the inefficacy of the subsisting federal government, you are called upon to deliberate on a new constitution for the United States of America. The subject speaks its own importance; comprehending in its consequences, nothing less than the existence of the UNION, the safety and welfare of the parts of which it is composed, the fate of an empire, in many respects, the most interesting in the world. It has been frequently remarked, that it seems to have been reserved to the people of this country, by their conduct and example, to decide the important question, whether societies of men are really capable or not, of establishing good government from reflection and choice, or whether they are forever destined to depend, for their political constitutions, on accident and force. If there be any truth in the remark, the crisis, at which we are arrived, may with propriety be regarded as the æra in which

A   that

The Federalist Papers first appeared in New York newspapers in 1787 and 1788. All the essays are still available in book form as *The Federalist Papers*.

Writing the Constitution was hard. Getting the states to approve it was even harder. James Madison, Alexander Hamilton of New York, and others worried that their work might end up in the wastebasket. So they wrote essays supporting the Constitution. These eighty-five essays, printed in newspapers throughout the states, are called the Federalist Papers. (People who supported the Constitution were called *Federalists.* People who were against it were called *anti-Federalists.*) Madison and Hamilton were pretty persuasive. Their essays helped convince all states to ratify (approve) the Constitution by 1788. The essays still make for good reading.

"**SOUND** "Tis done! . . .
BYTE" We have
become a nation."
—Benjamin Rush,
after ratification
of the
Constitution
in 1788

Article VII also says the Constitution doesn't have to be approved by each state's legislature. Instead, the states would hold conventions to ratify the Constitution. The people of each state would elect convention delegates. And in less than a year, the people's final decision would be clear. They chose to ratify the Constitution.

Congress of the United States.

begun and held at the City of New York,

on Wednesday the fourth of March one thousand seven hundred and eighty nine.

CHAPTER 4
DON'T FORGET THE BILL OF RIGHTS

QUICK QUESTION: What's a bill of rights? In the 1780s, each state had its own document stating the rights of people. People might have the right to a quick and fair trial. They might have the right to worship in the church of their choice. Or they might have the right to state their opinions in the press.

A bill of rights protects people from tyrants. What's a tyrant? A tyrant is a ruler who has complete power and uses

The Bill of Rights, the first ten amendments (additions) to the Constitution, outlines the basic rights of U.S. citizens.

it in cruel and unjust ways. A bill of rights is designed to stop tyrants and to guarantee the rights of all people.

In 1788 some states were refusing to ratify the Constitution if a bill of rights wasn't added to it. George Washington agreed. When he spoke at his inauguration (swearing-in ceremony as president) in 1789, he asked Congress to start proposing amendments to the Constitution. Those amendments would give Americans their bill of rights.

In March 1789, James Madison arrived in New York

On his inauguration day, President Washington greeted enthusiastic crowds.

for the first session of Congress. He read newspapers and cut out articles about proposed amendments to the Constitution. To this scrapbook, he added all the amendments states had suggested when they had ratified the Constitution. It was a long list, covering everything from freedom of religion to limiting presidents to one term in office.

"ALL HAIL HIS HIGHNESS THE PRESIDENT!"

Writing the Bill of Rights wasn't the only important work done by the first session of Congress. Members also debated what to call George Washington, the new president. Should he be called, as some suggested, "His Highness the President of the United States and Protector of Their Liberties"? After much talk, the House and Senate agreed on something simpler: the president of the United States.

RATIFIED RIGHTS

By early June, Madison had narrowed down the list to nine amendments. That list, along with eight more amendments proposed by other members of the House, went to the Senate. The Senate then whittled it down to twelve. Those amendments were officially proposed on September 25, 1789. But only ten of the twelve were ratified by the states. Those ten, ratified in December of 1791, became the first ten amendments to the U.S.

Did You KNOW? The copy of the Bill of Rights on display in Washington, D.C., actually includes twelve amendments—the first two, which weren't ratified, and the remaining ten amendments, which were.

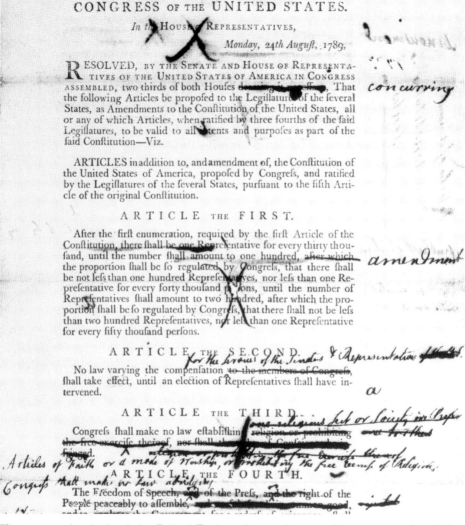

This copy of a draft of the Bill of Rights shows changes that were made while members of the House of Representatives discussed it.

Constitution, known as the Bill of Rights.

The Bill of Rights makes clear our rights as citizens of the United States. Think back to why Americans wanted to be independent from Britain, and it's easy to see why certain rights are spelled out in the Bill of Rights.

The First Amendment says Congress can never set up a state religion. (Remember how America was founded by people seeking freedom of religion?) It also says Congress can never pass laws that will make printers afraid to print the news. (Remember how colonial presses were shut down if they criticized the king?)

The Second Amendment says states need well-armed militias. But the Third Amendment adds that "no soldier shall, in time of peace be quartered in any house, without

Before the Revolutionary War, British troops destroyed newspapers that were critical of colonial officials. Freedom of the press was an important right in the new United States.

Parliament allowed British troops to live in colonists' homes without the colonists' consent. This practice was not permitted under the new U.S. Constitution.

the consent of the owner, nor in time of war, but in a manner to be prescribed by law." In other words, citizens can't be forced to house soldiers. (Remember how much the colonists hated it when Britain stationed troops in their cities and forced people to open their homes to the redcoats?)

Americans remembered with bitterness how colonists' houses had been searched for tea. So the Fourth Amendment talks of "the right of the people to be secure in their persons, houses, papers, and effects, against unreasonable searches and seizures. . . . "

Several amendments protect the rights of Americans accused of crimes. The Fifth Amendment says Americans never have to testify (give evidence) against themselves in court. Under the Sixth and Seventh Amendments, Americans have "the right to a speedy and public trial, by an impartial [fair] jury. . . . " The Eighth Amendment says the courts can't ask for "excessive bail." (Bail is money you pay to the courts while you await trial. Once you pay bail, you can leave jail until your trial.)

MAY I ADD SOMETHING, PLEASE?

Several amendments have been made to the Constitution since it was written in 1787. More are bound to be added in the future. Twenty-seven amendments (including the ten called the Bill of Rights) have been passed as of 2003. They've added or strengthened important rights.

If you'd like to add something, write an amendment of your own. But give yourself plenty of time to get it passed. Generally speaking, you'll need two-thirds of Congress to go along with you to propose an amendment. Then you'll need to get at least three-quarters of the states to agree to the amendment.

The same amendment states that if found guilty, criminals won't suffer "cruel and unusual punishments."

The last two amendments in the Bill of Rights talk about what's *not* in the Constitution. The Ninth Amendment indicates that rights not mentioned in the Constitution belong to the people. Even if you don't see a particular right listed, it may still be protected. The Tenth Amendment says that when the Constitution does not give a specific power to the government of the United

The U.S. Capitol houses Congress, a vital part of the democratic system set up by the Declaration of Independence, the Constitution, and the Bill of Rights.

States, then that power belongs to the states or to the people. Many states worried that they would have no rights or powers left under the new Constitution. The Tenth Amendment reassures those worried states.

Do This!

What rights are most important to you? Could you write your own bill of rights? How would it differ from the U.S. Bill of Rights?

Each amendment in the Bill of Rights is short. Try reading one a day for ten days. The doctor couldn't make a better prescription for becoming a good citizen.

The democratic government set forth in the Declaration of Independence, the U.S. Constitution, and the Bill of Rights isn't perfect, but it has lasted more than two hundred years. More than just pieces of paper and parchment, these documents are the best road maps around to government by the people and for the people, and to liberty and justice for all.

A Timeline of Independence

1765   The British Parliament passes a tax on paper goods called the Stamp Act.

1766   After American colonists protest it, the Stamp Act is repealed.

1773   In protest of a tax the British placed on tea, colonists dump tea into Boston Harbor at the Boston Tea Party.

1774   British Parliament passes a series of laws the colonists call the Intolerable Acts. The First Continental Congress meets in Philadelphia in September.

1775   The first shots of the Revolutionary War are fired in the towns of Lexington and Concord in Massachusetts.

1776   Thomas Paine's *Common Sense* is published. The Declaration of Independence is drafted and then signed on July 4, breaking the colonies' ties with Britain. In December General George Washington leads his troops across the Delaware River and surprises the British at Trenton, New Jersey.

1777–1778   Washington's troops spend a cold winter at Valley Forge, Pennsylvania.

1781 The Articles of Confederation, an early framework for America's government, are approved in March. In October the British surrender to the Americans at the Battle of Yorktown in Virginia, ending the fighting in the Revolutionary War.

1783 The British and Americans sign a treaty to end the Revolutionary War.

1786 Facing tough economic times, angry farmers revolt during Shays's Rebellion, which ends in 1787.

1787 The U.S. Constitution is written.

1788 The U.S. Constitution is ratified, or approved, and becomes law.

1789 George Washington becomes the first president of the United States. The first amendments to the Constitution are proposed.

1791 The Bill of Rights, consisting of the first ten amendments to the Constitution, is ratified.

GLOSSARY

amendment: an addition that completes, changes, or corrects the original

Articles of Confederation: the document outlining the alliance formed in 1781 by the thirteen former British colonies in North America. This document also spells out the powers of the central government (the Confederation congress) and of the thirteen states under the alliance.

charter: a document on paper, papyrus, or parchment, usually granting specific rights to the people of a nation

Charters of Freedom: the three documents—the Declaration of Independence, Constitution, and Bill of Rights—that define American democracy

constitution: the broad outlines of a government

Continental Congress: at first, a meeting of delegates from the thirteen British colonies in North America in 1774. Gradually, the Continental Congress became the first central government of the United States.

Declaration of Independence: the official announcement, signed July 4, 1776, of the United States's intention to break ties with its former colonial ruler, Great Britain, and form a new government

delegate: someone who stands for others, acting on their behalf, at a convention or conference. Nearly all of the thirteen states, for example, sent delegates to the Constitutional Convention held in 1787.

draft: an early version of a text, meant to be polished and revised

executive branch: that part of the U.S. government that includes the president, vice president, presidential staff, advisers, and cabinet members

judicial branch: that part of the U.S. government that includes the federal courts and the U.S. Supreme Court

legislative branch: the lawmaking part of the U.S. government, made up of two houses: the House of Representatives and the Senate

mercenaries: professional soldiers who fight for pay, serving various governments at different times

parchment: specially treated goat, pig, or cow skin used for writing upon

parliament: a lawmaking body. In Great Britain, Parliament passes laws.

petition: a written document making a formal request to a governing body or to a superior

ratify: to approve

repealed: officially revoked, or ended

representative: someone who stands for others, acting on their behalf. In the U.S. House of Representatives, for example, members act on behalf of the citizens who elected them, giving those citizens representation in the government's lawmaking body.

senator: a person who acts on behalf of citizens of a state or other locale. The citizens of each state elect two senators to serve in the U.S. Senate.

tyrant: a ruler, such as a king, who holds total power over the people and uses power in cruel ways

U.S. Bill of Rights: the first ten amendments to the U.S. Constitution. In general, a bill of rights is a document outlining the freedoms guaranteed to citizens.

Source Notes

Unless otherwise noted below, all quotations are from the Charters of Freedom—the Declaration of Independence, the Constitution, and the Bill of Rights.

For quoted material: p. 10, Alfred F. Young, Terry J. Fife, and Mary E. Janzen, *We the People: Voices and Images of the New Nation* (Philadelphia: Temple University Press, 1993), 35; p. 12 left, Thomas Paine, *Common Sense, The Rights of Man, and Other Essential Writings of Thomas Paine* (New York: A Meridian Book, 1969), 48; p. 12 right, Thomas Paine quoted in Gordon S. Wood, *The American Revolution* (New York: Modern Library, 2002), 55; p. 13, Pauline Maier, *American Scripture: Making the Declaration of Independence* (New York: Knopf, 1997), 33; p. 16 left, Thomas Paine, *Common Sense*, 75; p. 16 right, Richard Henry Lee quoted in Robert Middlekauff, *The Glorious Cause: The American Revolution, 1763–1789* (New York: Oxford University Press, 1982), 325; p. 19, Elizabeth Cady Stanton quoted in Young, *We the People*, 224 (emphasis added); p. 21, Robert Allen Rutland, *The Birth of the Bill of Rights, 1776–1791*, rev. ed. (Boston: Northeastern University Press, 1983), 80; p. 27, George Washington quoted in Robert Allen Rutland, *James Madison: The Founding Father* (New York: Macmillan Publishing Company, 1987), 5; p. 28, Edmund Randolph quoted in Richard B. Morris, *Witnesses at the Creation: Hamilton, Madison, Jay, and the Constitution* (New York: Holt, Rinehart and Winston, 1985), 200; p. 33, Franklin D. Roosevelt quoted in Michael Kammen, ed., *The Origins of the American Constitution: A Documentary History* (New York: Penguin Books, 1986), vii; p. 36, Benjamin Rush quoted in *Voting Record of the Constitutional Convention, 1787*, <www.archives.gov/exhibit_hall/american_originals_iv/sections/nonjavatext_voting_record.html>; p. 39, Rutland, *James Madison*, 60.

BIBLIOGRAPHY

The Bill of Rights. Washington, D.C.: National Archives and Records Administration, 1986.

Bruns, Roger A. *A More Perfect Union: The Creation of the United States Constitution.* Washington, D.C.: National Archives and Records Administration, 1986.

Currie, David P. *The Constitution of the United States: A Primer for the People.* Chicago: University of Chicago Press, 1988.

Kammen, Michael, ed. *The Origins of the American Constitution: A Documentary History.* New York: Penguin Books, 1986.

Lucey, Donna. *I Dwell in Possibility: Women Build a Nation, 1600–1920.* Washington, D.C.: National Geographic Society Books, 2001.

Maier, Pauline. *American Scripture: Making the Declaration of Independence.* New York: Knopf, 1997.

Middlekauff, Robert. *The Glorious Cause: The American Revolution, 1763–1789.* New York: Oxford University Press, 1982.

Morris, Richard B. *Witnesses at the Creation: Hamilton, Madison, Jay, and the Constitution.* New York: Holt, Rinehart and Winston, 1985.

Paine, Thomas. *Common Sense, The Rights of Man, and Other Essential Writings of Thomas Paine.* 1776. Reprint, New York: A Meridian Book, 1969.

Rutland, Robert Allen. *The Birth of the Bill of Rights, 1776–1791.* Rev. ed. Boston: Northeastern University Press, 1983.

_____. *James Madison: The Founding Father.* New York: Macmillan Publishing Company, 1987.

Wood, Gordon S. *The American Revolution.* New York: Modern Library, 2002.

Young, Alfred F., Terry J. Fife, and Mary E. Janzen. *We the People: Voices and Images of the New Nation.* Philadelphia: Temple University Press, 1993.

FURTHER READING AND WEBSITES

Amstel, Marsha. *Sybil Ludington's Midnight Ride.* Minneapolis: Carolrhoda Books, Inc., 2000.

Blumer, Ronald. *Liberty! The American Revolution.* Alexandria, VA: PBS Video, 1997. Videorecording in six volumes.

Bohannon, Lisa Fredericksen. *The American Revolution.* Minneapolis: Lerner Publications Company, 2004.

Caltrow, David. *We the Kids.* New York: Dial Books for Young Readers, 2002.

Collier, James Lincoln, and Christopher Collier. *My Brother Sam Is Dead.* New York: Four Winds Press, 1974.

Day, Nancy. *Your Travel Guide to Colonial America.* Minneapolis: Runestone Press, 2001.

Feldman, Ruth Tenzer. *How Congress Works: A Look at the Legislative Branch.* Minneapolis: Lerner Publications Company, 2004.

Fink, Sam. *The Declaration of Independence.* New York: Scholastic Reference, 2002.

Fleming, Candace. *The Hatmaker's Sign.* Illustrated by Robert Andrew Parker. New York: Orchard, 1998.

Forbes, Esther. *Johnny Tremain.* Boston: Houghton Mifflin, 1943.

Freedman, Russell. *Give Me Liberty! The Story of the Declaration of Independence.* New York: Holiday House, 2000.

Fritz, Jean. *Shh! We're Writing the Constitution.* Illustrated by Tomie dePaola. New York: G. P. Putnam's Sons, 1987.

Hakim, Joy. *From Colonies to Country.* 2d ed. New York: Oxford University Press, 1999.

Hamilton, Alexander, and others. *The Federalist Papers.* Edited by Clinton Rossiter. New York: Mentor, 1999.

Hoose, Phillip. *We Were There, Too!: Young People in U.S. History.* New York: Melanie Kroupa Books, 2002.

Kowalski, Kathiann M. *Order in the Court: A Look at the Judicial Branch.* Minneapolis: Lerner Publications Company, 2004.

Krull, Kathleen. *A Kid's Guide to America's Bill of Rights: Curfews, Censorship, and the 100-pound Giant.* Illustrated by Anna DiVito. New York: Avon Books, 1999.

Landau, Elaine. *The President's Work: A Look at the Executive Branch.* Minneapolis: Lerner Publications Company, 2004.

McPherson, Elaine Marie. *Liberty or Death: A Story about Patrick Henry.* Minneapolis: Carolrhoda Books, Inc., 2003.

Meltzer, Milton. *The Bill of Rights: How We Got It and What It Means.* New York: Thomas Y. Crowell, 1990.

Miller, Brandon Marie. *Growing Up in Revolution and the New Nation 1775 to 1800.* Minneapolis: Lerner Publications Company, 2003.

Mitchell, Barbara. *Father of the Constitution: A Story about James Madison.* Minneapolis: Carolrhoda Books, Inc., 2004.

Ransom, Candace. *George Washington.* Minneapolis: Lerner Publications Company, 2002.

Roop, Peter, and Connie Roop. *Buttons for General Washington.* Minneapolis: Carolrhoda Books, Inc., 1986.

Sherrow, Victoria. *Benjamin Franklin.* Minneapolis: Lerner Publications Company, 2002.

_____. *Thomas Jefferson.* Minneapolis: Lerner Publications Company, 2002.

Waxman, Laura Hamilton. *Uncommon Revolutionary: A Story about Thomas Paine.* Minneapolis: Carolrhoda Books, Inc., 2004.

Weidt, Maryann N. *Revolutionary Poet: A Story about Phillis Wheatley.* Minneapolis: Carolrhoda Books, Inc., 1997.

Wister, Sarah. *A Colonial Quaker Girl: The Diary of Sally Wister, 1777–1778.* Mankato, MN: Blue Earth Books, 2000.

Zemlicka, Shannon. *Nathan Hale: Patriot Spy.* Minneapolis: Carolrhoda Books, Inc., 2002.

WEBSITES

Charters of Freedom Exhibit
<http://archives.gov/exhibit_hall/charters_of_freedom/charters_of_freedom.html>
This National Archives website showcases the Charters of Freedom: the Declaration of Independence, the U.S. Constitution, and the Bill of Rights.

National Constitution Center
<http://www.constitutioncenter.org>
At this website, you can take a virtual tour of the National Constitution Center in Philadelphia, search an interactive Constitution, explore the Constitution by topic, or print a copy of the Constitution.

INDEX

ABOUT THE AUTHOR

Gwenyth Swain is the author of more than twenty books for young readers, including biographies of Johnny Appleseed, William Penn, Elizabeth Cady Stanton, and Levi Coffin, all published by Carolrhoda Books, Inc. Her first work of historical fiction, the picture book *I Wonder As I Wander*, with illustrations by Ronald Himler, was published by Eerdmans Books for Young Readers. Her first middle-grade novel—*Chig and the Second Spread*—was published by Delacorte Press. Ms. Swain is also the author of juvenile biographies of Dred and Harriet Scott and Chief Little Crow, published by the Minnesota Historical Society Press. Swain was graduated Phi Beta Kappa, with majors in history and French, from Grinnell College. She lives and works as a writer in Saint Paul, Minnesota. For more about her and her books, go to <www.childrensliteraturenetwork.org/authors/swain.html>.

PHOTO ACKNOWLEDGMENTS

The photographs in this book are reproduced with the permission of: © Bettmann/CORBIS, pp. 4, 37, 40; © North Wind Picture Archives, pp. 6, 7 (both), 9, 14, 16, 17, 19, 21, 23, 27, 28, 29, 35, 41, 42; Peter Newark's American Pictures, pp. 8. 10, 15, 18, 22 (top), 25, 26, 38; Library of Congress, pp. 11 (LC-USZ62-8623), 34 (LC-USZC4-2541); The Art Archive/Gripsholm Castle Sweden/Dagli Orti, p. 12; © Brown Brothers, pp. 13, 22 (bottom); The Art Archive/Chateau de Blerancourt/Dagli Orti, p. 20; © Alan Schein Photography/CORBIS, p. 44. The illustration on p. 32 is by Bill Hauser.